T0114711

DON'T LEAVE HOME WITHOUT POWER

DR. FRANCIS A. RUNDLES

WESTBOW
PRESS®
A DIVISION OF THOMAS NELSON
& ZONDERVAN

This book is a work of non-fiction. Unless otherwise noted, the author and the publisher make no explicit guarantees as to the accuracy of the information contained in this book and in some cases, names of people and places have been altered to protect their privacy.

WestBow Press books may be ordered through booksellers or by contacting:

WestBow Press
A Division of Thomas Nelson & Zondervan
1663 Liberty Drive
Bloomington, IN 47403
www.westbowpress.com
844-714-3454

Because of the dynamic nature of the Internet, any web addresses or links contained in this book may have changed since publication and may no longer be valid. The views expressed in this work are solely those of the author and do not necessarily reflect the views of the publisher, and the publisher hereby disclaims any responsibility for them.

Any people depicted in stock imagery provided by Getty Images are models, and such images are being used for illustrative purposes only.
Certain stock imagery © Getty Images.

Scripture quotations marked NIV are taken from The Holy Bible, New International Version®, NIV® Copyright © 1973, 1978, 1984, 2011 by Biblica, Inc.® Used by permission. All rights reserved worldwide.

Scripture quotations marked KJV are taken from the King James Version. Public domain.

ISBN: 978-1-6642-9990-0 (sc)
ISBN: 978-1-6642-9991-7 (e)

Library of Congress Control Number: 2023909003

Print information available on the last page.

WestBow Press rev. date: 5/16/2023

Acts 1:8, "Ye shall receive power." (KJV) Power, according to GK Dunamis, means more than strength or ability; it designates especially power in operation, in action. Luke in his Gospel and in Acts, emphasizes that the Holy Ghost power included the authority to drive out evil spirits and the anointing to heal the sick as the two essential signs accompanying the proclamation of the kingdom of God.

INTRODUCTION

In the day and times that we are living in, there are daily challenges that we face as believers. Some of the challenges facing the church are institutional, ethical, doctrinal, political, cultural, religion, and mental health (e.g., anxiety; depression; guilt and shame; substance abuse; trauma; low self-esteem). They go across different faith traditions, denominations, ethnic groups, and sectors of the population. The word of the Lord shares with us in Isaiah 41:10 (NIV), "So do not fear for I am with you; do not be dismayed, for I am your God. I will strengthen you and help you; I will uphold you with my righteous right hand." Jesus told His disciples not to leave Jerusalem until they received the gift of the Holy Spirit.

THE CHALLENGES WE FACE

JONAH 3:6-10 (KJV)

1. **Polarization and Divisions.** In the first wave of COVID, churches faced division over politics, masks, regathering, streaming services, and social distancing. Then polarization over vaccinations. These attitudes and views created division into two sharply contrasting groups with vastly different beliefs and opinions.
2. **Weariness Expanded.** We are all tired. Church leaders particularly feel the exhaustion of dealing with so many issues.
3. **Decision Fatigue.** The deterioration of the quality of decisions has been challenged during the earlier months of the pandemic and has continued.
4. **Hopelessness Pervasive.** Our hope is in Jesus.
5. **Confusion About the Path Forward.** Continue back as before or adjust and adapt to the new normal.
6. **Denominational Structures Destabilizing.** No Help!
7. **Rethink the Way we are Going Forward.**

The Holy Spirit is a gift that Jesus promised to every believer. It is given to everyone who will receive it because the promise is to the parents and the children and as many as the Lord God shall call (Acts 2:39) (KJV). The Holy Spirit is essential and vital to the life of a believer who has received Jesus Christ as his Lord and Savior. The gift the Father promised (Joel 2:28-29-KJV; Matthew 3:11-KJV) is the baptism in the Holy Spirit. The fulfillment of that promise is described as being "filled with the Holy Ghost" and is at times used interchangeably in Acts. Many prefer the rendering, "you will be baptized in the Holy Ghost." Jesus knew the importance of the disciples having it. He knew that the Holy Spirit would help the believer have the power to do the impossible. He knew that believers would need unlimited help, guidance, and comfort to accomplish His great commission. We as humans are limited in some areas, but with the power of the Holy Ghost, the limits are removed. Jesus sent His disciples into a very hostile world where the devil is the prince and power of the air, and they would need the supernatural power that the Holy Ghost brings. Acts 1:4 (KJV), "And, being assembled together with them, commanded them that they should not depart from Jerusalem, but wait for the promise of the Father, which Saith He, ye have heard of me."

THE GREAT COMMISSION

The King James version Matthew 28:18 (KJV), "And Jesus came and spake unto them, saying, All Power is given unto me in heaven and in earths." Verse 19 (KJV), "Go ye therefore, and teach all nations, baptizing them in the name of the Father, and of the Son, and of the Holy Ghost:" In order to carry out this great power to proclaim the gospel throughout the world. But first the disciples had to obey Jesus' command to wait for the promise of the Father, which is the power of the Holy Spirit at Pentecost. Matthew's gospel final words of Jesus have become known as the *Great Commission*. We find in them the churching marching orders. These words are Christ's Great Commission to all His followers of every generation. It states the goal, responsibility, and commissioning of the church's missionary task.

1. The church is to go into all the world and preach the gospel to all people.
2. The preaching of the gospel is centered on "repentance and remission (forgiveness) of sins." (Luke 24:47) (KJV), the promise of receiving "the gift of the Holy Ghost" (Acts 2:38) (KJV), and the exhortation to separate from this corrupt generation (Acts 2:40) (KJV) while waiting for the return of Jesus from heaven (Acts 3:19-20- KJV; 1 Thess 1:10-KJV).
3. The purpose is to make disciples, not just converts, who will observe Christ's commands.

4. Christ commands us to consecrate on reaching lost men and women.
5. Those who believe in Christ and the gospel to be baptized with water. This represents their covenant pledge to renounce immorality, the world, and their own sinful nature and totally commit themselves to Christ and His kingdom purposes. "Iron sharpeneth iron; so a man sharpeneth the countenance of his friend," Proverbs 27:17 (KJV). As the proper toll shapes and sharpens iron for its desired use, so a man sharpens his friend morally and intellectually by their personal friendship.
6. Christ will be with His obedient followers in the presence and power of the Holy Spirit. They are to go to all nations and witness only after they are "endued with power from on high," (Luke 24:49 KJV). The greatest assurance that a believer has is to know that the Lord is with us. At the end of Matthew 28:20 (KJV), "and lo, I am with you always, even unto the end of the world. Amen."

I AM WITH YOU

Matthew 28:20 (KJV), "Teaching them to observe all things whatsoever I have commanded you: and lo, am with you always, even unto the end of world. Amen."

The purpose of the local church is to make disciples of all kinds of people. Those who are evangelized and converted should then be baptized, attesting to their identification with Christ and the local body of believers. The final phase of the Great Commission is to train or teach disciples in Christian knowledge and for effective service. A church cannot choose one aspect of its responsibility and neglect the others. The Great Commission is a simple command with three steps— evangelism, baptism, and education.

The Great Commission is the strategy by which the church at Jerusalem drenched its community with the gospel. It is imperative that the believer have the power of the Holy Ghost. What an assurance and comfort to know that the Lord is always present with us. Jesus promised that His presence and authority would be with all believers who go forth to (Matthew 28:19, KJV) "teach all nations." Jesus is ever present with us in the person of the Holy Spirit (John 14:26, KJV) and through His word (John 12:23, KJV). No matter what your current condition is— weak, poor, humble, a feeling of unimportant— Jesus cares for you, watches with concern every detail of life's trials and struggles, and gives both the grace that is sufficient (2 Cor 12:9- KJV) and His presence to lead you home (Matt 12:10 KJV, Acts 18:10 KJV).

God is a refuge and strength, a very present help in times of trouble

(Psalm 46:1, KJV). This is the Christian's answer to every fear, every doubt, every trouble, every heartache, and every discouragement. God is with us and will be with us until the end. Therefore, we are to live godly lives as disciples and equip others to do the same. The power and ability to face the uncertainties and adversities of life are found in God. The beauty of God's grace is that even when you run, he knows where you are going. In fact, He will be there to greet you when you arrive.

EVERY BELIEVER NEED TO BE EMPOWERED BY THE HOLY GHOST

In the Gospel of Matthew 3:11 (KJV), "I indeed baptize you with water unto repentance: but he that cometh after me is mightier than I, whose shoes I am not worthy to bear: he shall baptize you with the Holy Ghost, and with fire …"

John teaches that the work of the coming Messiah will involve baptizing His followers with the Holy Spirit– a baptism that gives great power to live and witness for Christ. Jesus baptizing His followers with or in the Holy Ghost is the new sign by which to identify God's people. This was promised in Joel 2:28 (KJV) and reaffirmed after Christ's resurrection (Luke 24:49-KJV; Acts 1:4-8-KJV). This prediction was initially fulfilled on the day of Pentecost.

Jesus Christ's ministry of baptizing in the Holy Ghost is a continuing ministry throughout this present age. Jesus, Himself, is the one who baptizes His believers in the Holy Ghost. John 1:33 (KJV), "And I knew him not: but he that sent me to baptize with water, the same said unto me, upon whom thou shalt see the Spirit descending, and remaining on him, the same is he which baptizeth with the Holy Ghost." All four Gospels emphasize that Jesus is " …he which baptizeth with (in) the Holy Ghost" (Mat 3:11; Mark 1:8; Luke 3:16; John 1:33) (KJV). The Holy Ghost would be poured out upon them so that they might carry on His saving work in all the world.

Acts 1:8 is the key verse in the book of Acts. The primary purpose of the baptism in the Spirit is the receiving of power to witness for Christ, so that the lost will be won over to Him and taught to obey all that Christ commanded. The Holy Ghost will bring back to remembrance everything that Jesus said. The end result is that Christ may be known, loved, praised, and made Lord of the chosen people of the Lord.

Ye Shall Receive Power.

In verse 8,(KJV) "ye shall receive power.." Power means in the Greek, dunamis, which means more than strength or ability; it designates especially power in operation, in action. Luke in his Gospel and in Acts emphasizes that the Holy Spirit's power included the authority to drive out the devil and the anointing to heal the sick as the two essential signs. The release of the power of the Holy Ghost in Act in and through the believers' lives caused them to witness "with all boldness" (4:29) KJV, "with great power" (4:33) KJV, with many signs, wonders, and miracles.

Ye Shall be Witnesses.

The baptism in the Holy Ghost not only imparts power to preach Jesus as Lord and Savior, but also increases the effectiveness of that witness because of a strengthening and deepening relationship with the Father, Son, and Holy Ghost that comes from being filled with the Spirit. The Holy Ghost witnesses "righteousness" and "truth" which "glorify" Christ (John 16:8, 10, 13-14) KJV, not only with words, but also in deeds. So, we who have received the witness of the Spirit to Christ's redemptive work will necessarily manifest Christlikeness, love, truth, and righteousness in our lives (1 Cor 13). The baptism in the Holy Ghost is the initiation point whereby Spirit-filled believers receive the enabling power of the Spirit to witness for Christ and to be carriers of His life, hope, and forgiveness of sins to the lost so that sinners can be saved. The Holy Ghost comes into the hearts of those who are already saved. The Holy Ghost reveals and makes more real to us the personal presence of Jesus. Any witness to an intimate fellowship with Jesus Christ, Himself, will result in an ever-growing desire on our part to love, honor, and to please our Lord and Savior Jesus Christ. The Holy Ghost is called the Spirit of Truth. He is a helper, teacher, and comforter, by bringing to remembrance the things they may have forgotten. In this day of mental stress and anxiety, believers need the power of the Holy Ghost to deal with everyday pressures.

THE HOLY GHOST IS
THE ESSENTIAL THING

We are reminded in Acts 1:8, (KJV) "But ye shall receive power after that the Holy Ghost has come upon you." The whole Armour of God; 6:10 From now on it will be all out war. 6:11 The devil carefully devises schemes and tactics against you– Spiritual Warfare.

Wrestle means it is personal, Ephesians 6:12.

Wherefore means because of this– 2 Corinthians 10:4,(KJV) "For the weapons of our warfare are not carnal, but mighty through God to the pulling down of strongholds;" Ephesians 6:13.

2 Corinthians 10:5,(KJV) "Casting down imaginations, and every high thing that exalteth itself against the knowledge of God, and bringing into captivity every thought to the obedience of Christ;"

Ephesians 6:14-17, the whole armor of God consists of six pieces:

1. They are the truth.
2. The breastplate of righteousness.
3. Preparation of the gospel of peace.
4. The shield of faith.
5. The helmet of salvation.
6. The sword of the Spirit, which is the word of God.

Ephesians 6:18. Praying is grammatically linked to "stand" in verse 14. Without prayer, God's armor is inadequate to achieve victory. Prayer is indispensable. Always means "on every occasion, that is when Satan attacks in the Spirit …"

Watching thereunto means being vigilant, or alert, in this very matter of prayer. They are to pray not just for themselves but also for all saints. Spiritual combat is both an individual and corporate matter. The Lord shall lift up His standard against the enemy. God's arm brought forth salvation, and His righteousness sustained it.

A POWERLESS CHURCH

The results of leaving home without power caused the disciples to not be able to heal a demonic boy. In Matthew's Gospel chapter 17:14-21, this text reflects Jesus' estimation of disciples and churches who fail to minister to others in the real power of God's kingdom. Failure to deliver those oppressed by Satan or demons demonstrates a lack of faith, understanding, and spiritual authority. The Holy Spirit's purpose in recording Matthew 17:14-21 narrative is to emphasize not only that Jesus drove out demons, but also that He desires His disciples to do the same thing through faith. Jesus is intensely disappointed and pained when His people fail to share in His ministry against the forces of Satan. Jesus wants His followers to wage war against the forces of Evil by driving out evil spirits and healing the sick. This demonstration of authority in spiritual confrontation is the continuing manifestation of the kingdom of God on Earth. Failure to wage effective warfare against demons is seen as spiritual weakness on the part of Christ's disciples.

In the Gospel of Mark Chapter 9:28-29 (KJV), "And when he was come into the house his disciples asked him privately, why could not we cast him out? And he said unto them, This kind can come forth by nothing, but by prayer and fasting." Jesus does not mean that a time out for prayer was necessary before this kind of evil spirit could be driven out, rather a principle is implied here: Where there is little faith, there is little prayer. Littler prayer, little power, no prayer, no power. When there is much prayer and intimacy with God coupled together with a life of love and obedience to God and His word, there is much faith and spiritual authority. Had the disciples been maintaining, as Jesus did, a life of prayer, they could have dealt successfully with this issue; that is, a faith that can move mountains, cause miracles and healing, and accomplish great things for God. Faith produces results; it shall move mountains.

RECEIVING THE GIFT
OF THE HOLY GHOST

"And when the day of Pentecost was fully come, they were all with one accord in one place. And suddenly there came a sound from heaven as of a rushing mighty wind, and it filled the house where they were sitting. And there appeared unto them cloven tongues like as of fire, and it sat upon each of them. And they were all filled with the Holy Ghost, and began to speak with other tongues, as the Spirit gave them utterance," Acts 2:1-4 (KJV).

Pentecost was a great festival of the Jewish year. It was a harvest festival where the first fruits of the grain harvest were presented to God. At Pentecost, there were three manifestations that the Holy Spirit descended upon the 120 in the upper room. There was a sound " ...as a rushing mighty wind," (v.2) KJV as a prophetic sign that the Holy Ghost is coming in "Power".

1. Manifestation is audible
2. Manifestation is visual
3. Manifestation is speech

As the 120 were being "filled with the Holy Ghost," they began to speak with other tongues. On this occasion it was in different languages and understood by the different nations represented in the crowd. The pouring out of the Holy Ghost by Jesus proves that He indeed is the exalted

Messiah, now sitting at the right hand of God and interceding for His spoken persons on earth.

"Therefore being by the right hand of God exalted, and having received of the Father the promise of the Holy Ghost, he hath shed forth this, which ye now see and hear," Acts 2:33 (KJV).

From Jesus' baptism onward the Spirit was fully upon Him as the Christ that is, the one anointed by the Spirit. Now He is at the right hand of the Father, He lives to pour out the same Spirit upon those who believe in Him. By receiving the gift of the Holy Ghost, Jesus intends that the Spirit will mediate Jesus' presence to believers and empower them to continue to do all that He did while on earth. One of the criteria of receiving the gift of the Holy Ghost is that you must repent. Repent means to change one's mind. In verse chapter 2 verse 38 of the Book of Acts, repentance, forgiveness of sins, and baptism are the prior conditions for receiving the gift of the Holy Ghost. However, Peter's demand that his hearers be baptized in water before receiving the promise of the Father must not be taken as an absolute requirement for the infilling with the Spirit, nor is baptism in the Spirit an automatic consequence of water baptism. Acts 2:39 (KJV), "For the promise is unto you, and to your children, and to all that are afar off, even as many as the Lord our God shall call." The promise of the baptism in the Holy Ghost was not just for those person's present on the day of Pentecost, but for all who believe in Christ throughout this age.

Prayer is essential to a strong faith in Christ Jesus. In the early church, prayer was clearly a high priority and an integral part of their life together. In Acts, where there is much prayer, there is a mighty move of the Holy Ghost. Miracles, signs, and wonders happen due to a praying people of God. Miracles were an important aspect of the presence and power of the Holy Ghost among believers and occurred most often in their mission to unbelievers. In Acts 3:6, the healing of the cripple man was done by the power of the Holy Ghost working through the disciples. Jesus said to His followers concerning those who would believe in Him, "In my name they shall lay hands on the sick, and they shall recover," Mark 16:17-18 (KJV). The miracle was accomplished through faith in the name of Jesus Christ "and gifts of healing" operating through Peter. Peter tells him that he had no money, but what he would give him is something so much better. "In the name of Jesus Christ of Nazareth rise up and walk," Acts 3:6 (KJV).

"And he took him by the right hand, and lifted him up: and immediately his feet and ankle bones received strength," Acts 3:7 (KJV). In verse 19 of Acts chapter 3, God has chosen to bless His people with the outpouring of the Holy Ghost only on the conditions of repentance, that is, turning from sin and the unrighteous ways of their surrounding corrupt generation, and conversion, that is turning to God and always move towards sincere obedience to Christ.

FILLED WITH THE HOLY GHOST

In Acts 4:8 (KJV), "Then Peter, filled with the Holy Ghost, said unto them, and elders Israel ..." Peter received a fresh filling with the Holy Ghost. The Holy Ghost brought a sudden inspiration, wisdom, and boldness by which to proclaim the truth of God. It is significant theologically that the filling with the Spirit was not a one-time experience, but a repetitive one. This is a fulfillment of Jesus' promise in the Gospel of Luke 12:11-12; other renewed fillings can be found in Acts 7:55 and 13:9. Without the power of the Holy Ghost, we cannot speak the things of God. The Holy Ghost created in the apostles an overwhelming desire to proclaim the gospel. Throughout this book of Acts, the Spirit empowered believers to carry the gospel to others. Acts 4:31 (KJV), "And when they had prayed, the place was shaken where they were assembled together; and they were all filled with the Holy Ghost, and they spake the word of God with boldness." The Spirit here visits a whole congregation; therefore, to be able to fulfill the will of God, the church, not only must believers be filled with the Spirit, but also their entire congregations should experience repeated visitations of the Holy Ghost when special needs and challenges are present. God's moving upon the entire congregation with a renewed filling of the Holy Ghost results in boldness and power in witness, love for one another, and abundant grace for all. The inner power of the Spirit and the reality of God's presence brought about the filling of the Spirit to free the believers from fear of others and it increases the courage to speak for God.

In chapter 5 of the Book of Acts, Ananias and Sapphira, his wife, were punished for lying to the Holy Ghost. In order to gain glory and recognition, Ananias and Sapphira lied to the church about their giving. God considered this lie against the Holy Ghost a serious offense. This death of Ananias and Sapphire are intended to be standing examples of God's attitude toward any deceitful heart among those who profess to be saved and are born-again, spirit-filled believers. In actuality they were lying to God. The root of this sin was their love for money and for the praise of men. Many give to be seen and not from the abundance of the heart. This set them against the Holy Ghost. Once the love of money and human praise takes possession of a person, his or her spirit becomes open to all kinds of satanic evil.

I Timothy 6:10 (KJV), "For the love of money is the root of all evil: which while some coveted after, they have erred from the faith, and pierced themselves through with many sorrows." A person cannot love money and at the same time love and serve God. In verse 5,10 God harshly struck down Ananias and Sapphira in order to reveal His hatred of all deceit and dishonesty in the Kingdom of God. One of the most detestable sins in the church is to deceive God's people about our relationship with Christ, your work for Him, and the extent of your ministry. To engage in this hypocrisy means using Christ's shed blood to glorify your own self before other people. This sin disregards the very purpose for which Christ suffered and died. God's judgment upon the sin of Ananias and Sapphira caused an increase in humility, awe, and fear. Without a proper fear of the holy God and His wrath against sin, God's people will soon return to the ungodly ways of the world and cease to experience the outpouring of the Holy Ghost. The fear of the Lord is the essential part in the New Testament faith.

LOOKING FOR QUALIFIED MEN

In the Pentecostal churches, any person will be admitted as a candidate for membership of the local church when such person expresses a willingness to be saved from his or her sins and become subject to the doctrine of the church. It is then the duty of the pastor or a person appointed by the pastor to conduct a new member class with emphasis on how to be filled with the Holy Ghost. Appointment of positions in the Pentecostal church, were based on that individual having the Holy Ghost. As part of the leadership of the church, they are expected to support the church with tithing and offerings, regular attendance, and remain in good standing with the church leadership. As seen in chapter 6 of the Book of Acts, seven men were appointed, but the prerequisite was that they must be full of the Holy Ghost. The apostles stipulated that the seven men had to give evidence of having continued faithfully under the influence of the Holy Ghost. Apparently, the apostles assumed that not all believers continued to be full of the Spirit. In other words, those who fail to live faithfully by the Spirit will cease to be full of the Spirit. Acts 6:4 (KJV) states, "But we will give ourselves continually to prayer, and to the ministry of the word." Baptism in the Holy Ghost alone is insufficient for effective Christian leadership. Church leaders must constantly devote themselves to prayer and to the preaching of the Word. The apostles felt that prayer and the ministry of the word were the highest work of Christian leaders. One of the men that was consecrated to serve was Stephen who was a man of spiritual power. Acts 6:8 (KJV) explains in more detail about Stephen's character, "And Stephen, full of faith and power, did great wonders and miracles among the people." The Holy Ghost empowered Stephen to perform "great wonders and miracles among the people" and give him great wisdom to preach the gospel in such a way that his enemies could not refute his belief.

WHO IS ELIGIBLE TO RECEIVE THE HOLY GHOST?

"A devout man, and one that feared God with all his houses," Acts 10:2 (KJV). That man was named Cornelius, a centurion Roman military officer who was in charge of about one hundred men. He was a Gentile that feared God, who stopped serving idols and saw something better in the word of God that he heard in the Jewish synagogues. He didn't submit to Jewish circumcision or the ritual washings required of full Jewish proselytes, but he believed in Yahweh and worshiped Him. Cornelius and the people with whom came to be known as God-fearers. Cornelius has been fasting and praying and sees a vision and angel telling him that his prayers have been answered. He tells him of Peter, who is staying with Simon, a tanner. The next day Peter is praying and becomes very hungry, but he falls off in a trance. During this time, God shows him all manner of four-footed beast and wild beast, creeping things, and birds that are not lawful for him to eat. Acts 10:13 (KJV), "And there came a voice to him, Rise, Peter: kill and eat." Peter replies and says, "Not so, Lord; for I have never eaten anything that is common or unclean," 10:14 (KJV).

So, who is eligible? God uses the vision of the sheet to teach Peter two truths:

1. God has now cleansed all animals for food, contrary to the dietary code of the Mosaic Law.
2. All men of any ethnic background are fit for salvation.

God has no favorite nation or ethnic group, nor does He favor any individual because of nationality, birth, or position in life. God only favors those from every nation who turn from sin, believe in Christ, fear God, and live righteously. Everyone who continues in this way of life will remain in God's love and favor. God is no respecter of persons. While Peter preached to them, the Holy Ghost fell on the Gentiles like it fell on them, and because of the acceptance of Christ by the Gentiles, God poured out His Spirit upon them also.

THE BAPTISM OF THE HOLY GHOST WITH FIRE!

In preparation for the coming ministry of the Savior on earth, John the Baptist, the forerunner of the Lord, announced as he was preaching in the wilderness. Matthew 3:11 (KJV), "I indeed baptize you with water unto repentance: but he that cometh after me is mightier than I, whose shoes I am not worthy to bear: he shall baptize you with the Holy Ghost, and with fire:" John teaches us that the work of the coming Messiah will involve baptizing believers with the Holy Ghost. A baptism that gives great power to live and witness for Christ. The use of the word 'fire' suggests that those who receive this gift with the right heart can expect something more than just being baptized in water.

The new convert, who has accepted the gift of the Holy Ghost with the right Spirit, will experience not only a cleansing, but a feeling that will give him a new heart and make him a new person. Sometimes this happens immediately and sometimes it takes awhile. But there is always a change for the better. For those long-standing members of the church who have become preoccupied with the world or in little ways has allowed his religious life to be more procedural than of the Spirit, there is a refilling of the Holy Ghost and fire. This was promised in Joel 2:28 and reaffirmed after Christ's resurrection. Initially, it was fulfilled on the day of Pentecost (Acts 2:4). Christ's ministry of baptizing in the Holy Ghost is a continuing ministry throughout this present age. When you know you have it, it is a light to your feet and lamp to your path; a joy to the soul, opening up the things of God; bearing witness of the truth of this work and that the spirit has led me to righteousness, to truth, to purity of character, and will rebuke me when I attempt to do anything wrong; encourage me in doing what's right. We need this power.

The miracle of the manifestation of the fire and the Holy Ghost has the capacity to reach within a person's heart. While that person may have been a bystander regarding the things of God, the power of the Holy Ghost is able to turn such a person into a living witness of this sacred work.

HAVING AN EAR TO
HEAR THE LEADING
OF THE HOLY GHOST

In Acts 13:2 (KJV), "As they ministered to the Lord, and fasted, the Holy Ghost said, separate me Barnabas and Saul for the work whereunto I have called them." Fasting and praying was the prerequisite for the spirit led church and ministers. Christ, Himself, practiced this discipline and taught that it should be a part of Christian devotion and an act of preparation for His coming back. Fasting with prayer has several purposes: (1) to honor God; (2) to humble ourselves before God in order to experience more grace and God's intimate presence; (3) to mourn over personal sin and failure; (4) to mourn over the sins of the church, nation, and world.

Spirit-filled Christians are especially sensitive to the communication of the Holy Ghost during prayer and fasting. Paul and Barnabas were called to spread the gospel to the nations and were commissioned to go by the church and the Holy Ghost; they were also called to preach the gospel, bringing men and women into a saving relationship with Christ. Nowhere do we find in scripture that they were sent to do social or political work, that is, to propagate the gospel and establish churches by political activities for the benefit of the Roman Empire. The charge was to bring souls to Christ, deliver them from the power of Satan, cause the Holy Ghost to come upon them, and establish them in churches. In these churches, Christians were given gifts by the Spirit to transform them from within so their lives would bring glory to Jesus.

The missionary principles described in Acts chapter 13 are a model for all missionary sending churches. Missionary activity is initiated by the Holy Ghost through spiritual leaders who are devoted to the Lord and His kingdom, seeking Him with prayer and fasting. The church must be sensitive to the leading of the Holy Ghost. Missionaries who go must not leave without the power of the Holy Ghost. By prayer and fasting, constantly seeking to be aligned with God's will, the church confirms those that God sets apart by the laying on of hands.

FORBIDDEN OF THE HOLY GHOST

ACTS 16:6-9

One of the great testimonies in the older Pentecostal church was the saying, "I am saved, sanctified and baptized with the Holy Ghost. The Holy Ghost leads and guides me every day." The saints of old didn't make a move without the leading of the Spirit of God. Paul and Silas were called to Macedonia but before then they made an attempt to swing down through the southern province of Asia; the Holy Ghost forbade them. They then attempted to turn back through the northern province of Bithynia, again the spirit stopped them. Every initiative in Evangelism and missionary activity, in the book of Acts, is the result of the leading of the Holy Ghost. The guidance may have taken the form of a prophetic revelation, inward prompting, outward circumstances or visions. Luke did not indicate why the spirit constrained Paul's plans, or by what method God made known the restrictions. God gave Paul a vision to communicate His will for the direction his ministry should take, just as He had done with Peter. Maybe the reason that Paul was restricted from preaching in Asia was due to the fact that God planned for him to evangelize Macedonia. Under the impulse of the Holy Spirit, believers moved forward to take the gospel to the lost or unsaved. When being led by the Spirit from going in one direction, they would go in another, trusting in the Holy Ghost to either approve or disapprove of their directions. "In all thy ways acknowledge him, and he shall direct thy paths," Proverbs 3:6 (KJV). In all our plans, decisions, and activities, we should follow the leading of the Holy Ghost.

THE HOLY GHOST IS THE ESSENTIAL THING IN SPIRITUAL WARFARE

2 Corinthians 10:4-5 (KJV), "For the weapons of our warfare are not carnal, but mighty through God to the pulling down of strongholds; Casting down imaginations, and every high thing that exalteth itself against the knowledge of God, and bringing into captivity every thought to the obedience of Christ;".

From now on it will be all out war because the devil carefully devises schemes and tactics against you. Satan is a masterful strategist who seeks our downfall by his various schemes. Some of "the wiles of the devil" are to perpetuate division in the church, unbelief in the promises of God, discouragement, temptation to sin, unwillingness to forgive, and taking our eyes off Jesus, fear, and so on. We can be assured that over two thousand and twenty-two years ago on a hill called Calvary, we received victory by Jesus Christ. At the present time we are involved in a spiritual warfare that we wage by the power of the Holy Ghost (Romans 8:13): against the sinful desires within ourselves (1 Peter 2:11), and against the ungodly pleasures of the world and temptations of every sort. It takes the power of the Holy Ghost to be successful in spiritual warfare. In this war as Christian soldiers, we must wage war against all evil, not in our own power but by the power of the Holy Ghost.

In our warfare of faith, we are called to endure hardships like good soldiers of Christ, suffer for the gospel, and fight the good fight of faith, wage war and persevere. One of the old testimony songs says, "believe I hold on and see what the end is going to be." We must continue in a course of action even in the face of difficulty. The word of God is our offensive weapon in spiritual warfare. Satan will make every effort to undermine or destroy our confidence in the word of God. In the books of Ephesians 6:18 (KJV), praying is grammatically linked to "stand" in verse 14 of the six chapters of Ephesians. Without prayer, God's armor is inadequate to achieve victory. Prayer is indispensable; we must pray in the Holy Ghost. Our warfare against the spiritual forces of Satan calls for an intensity in prayer, that is, praying in the Spirit always, "with all prayer and supplication, for all saints," "with all perseverance."

Prayer is to be in as part of the actual conflict itself, where the victory is won for ourselves and others by working together with God, Himself. To fail to pray diligently, with all kinds of prayer in all situations, is to surrender to the enemy. Much prayer, much power. Little prayer, little power. No prayer, no power. In the spirit in this text means, "being alert in this very matter of prayer." They are to pray not just for themselves but also for all saints. Spiritual combat is both an individual and corporate matter. Jude verse 20, (KJV) "But ye, beloved, building up yourselves on your most holy faith, praying in the Holy Ghost …" Believers must defend and cultivate the faith and resist false teaching. This requires study of God's word and a determined effort to know the truth and teaching of scripture. By praying in the Spirit, we must pray by the enabling power of the Holy Spirit to inspire, guide, energize, sustain and help us to do battle in our praying. Praying in the Spirit includes both praying with one's mind and praying with one's spirit.

DON'T LEAVE HOME WITHOUT POWER! LORD, PLEASE SEND A REFRESHING!

ACTS 3:19

"Repent ye therefore, and be converted, that your sins may be blotted out, when the times of refreshing shall come from the presence of the Lord;" Acts 3:19 (KJV). Repent … and be converted. Repent means to feel or express sincere regret or remorse about one's sin, which requires absolute, ultimate, and unconditional surrender to God as sovereign—a 180-degree turn. When we think of the word 'refreshing', a transitive verb, we think of when we are hot, tired, or thirsty; it makes you feel cooler or more energetic. Jeremiah 31:25 (NIV), "I will refresh the weary and satisfy the faint."

God has chosen to bless his people with the outpouring of the Holy Ghost only on the conditions of repentance, that is, turning from sin and the unrighteous ways of the surrounding corrupt generation. Conversion is turning to God, listening to everything that Christ, the Prophet, tells them, and always moving toward sincere obedience to Christ.

Throughout this present age and until Christ's return, God will send "times of refreshing," that is, the outpouring of the Holy Ghost to all who repent and are converted. Although perilous (dangerous), time will come toward the end of this age and a great falling away from the faith will occur, but God still promises to send revival and times of refreshing upon the faithful. Christ's presence, spiritual blessings, miracles, and outpourings of the Spirit will come upon the remnant who faithfully seek him and overcome the world, the sinful nature, and the dominion of Satan. "And he shall send Jesus Christ, which before was preached unto you:" Acts 3:20 (KJV). "I will refresh the weary and satisfy the faint," Psalm 23:1-3 (KJV).

"The Lord called to be a light in a dark world!" Acts 26:15-18 (KJV). Paul's divine commission reminds us to not quit. Ephesians 1:18 (KJV), "The eyes of your understanding being enlightened; that ye may know what is the hope of his calling, and what the riches of the glory of His inheritance in the saints."

Acts 22:15 (KJV), "For thou shalt be his witness unto all men of what thou hast seen and heard." Acts 26:16 wants us to stand up and be a witness. "Then the eyes of the blind shall be opened, and the ears of the deaf shall be unstopped," Isaiah 35:5 (KJV). To open the blind eyes, by His death and the power of the Holy Ghost, the Messiah would free all believers from the darkness of sin and guild and release them from the power of Satan. Lord, please send a refreshing! An outpouring of the Holy Ghost!

BEYOND
THE WATER

In the book of Acts chapter 19 verse 2, (KJV) Paul asked a question to 12 disciples of John. "Have ye received the Holy Ghost since ye believed?" There is deeper depth and higher heights in Christ Jesus. Paul's question here refers to the baptism in the Holy Ghost for power and ministry, the same as that which happened at Pentecost. It is unlikely that Paul would inquire whether they had received the Spirit's indwelling presence as believers, for Paul clearly knew from the very moment of their belief, conversion, and regeneration. The response of John's disciples does not mean they had never heard of the Holy Ghost. They were well acquainted with the Old Testament teaching about the Spirit, and must certainly have heard John's message concerning the baptism in the Holy Ghost that Christ was to bring. They had not yet heard that the Spirit was being poured out on believers. In verse 5, KJV "When they heard this they were baptized in the name of the Lord Jesus." Water baptism in "the name of the Lord Jesus" of these twelve people at Ephesus testifies that they had saving faith and were born again by the Spirit. This proceeds their being filled with the Holy Ghost in verse 6. They had believed in Jesus and were born again by the Spirit. After they were baptized in the water, Paul laid his hands on them and they were baptized in the Holy Ghost. As the Holy Ghost came upon them, it was signified as they began speaking in tongues and prophesying. Speaking in tongues was external and visible proof that the Holy Ghost had come upon the believer.

HAVE YOU RECEIVED
THE HOLY GHOST
SINCE YOU BELIEVE?

ACTS 19:2 KJV

Saints of God the question for the hours is have you received the Holy Ghost since you believed? Have you been baptized with the Holy Ghost? If the answer is no, now is time to ask God to fill you with the power of the Holy Ghost. We have to realize that it's time to move past being justified and let God sanctify us holy and fill us with His precious gift of the Holy Spirit. Yes, it is a beautiful thing that you are saved, this means that you have repented of your sins and have accepted Jesus Christ as your Lord and Savior. Hallelujah, Praise God for being saved is beautiful because this means God has called you out of darkness into His marvelous light–that if you died right now, you are on your way to heaven. Like, I teach my congregation, if God is going to keep up here any length of time, then we must have the Holy Ghost.

Why is it important that we be baptized with the Holy Ghost? Because the Holy Ghost is God and we need the spirit of God to be on the inside of us to make it through the trials and tribulations of life. When you are on the Lord's side, you're going to face persecution. This is why it's important to study the word and to have the Holy Ghost because the Holy Ghost is our comforter. The Holy Ghost is our lead and our guide, and the Holy Ghost is what brings back remembrance of what Jesus said when we need it the most. The Holy Ghost is what gives us strength to make it day by day. The Holy Ghost is what brings us into the full knowledge of who Jesus is. The Holy Ghost is what makes intercession for us when we pray. For the Bible says in Romans 8:26 (KJV), "Likewise the Spirit also helpeth our infirmities; for we know not what we should pray for as we ought: but the Spirit himself maketh intercession for us with groanings which cannot be uttered."

Saints were living in a time now that we cannot leave home without the Holy Ghost. In order for us to be effective witnesses for Christ, in order for us to be ready to combat the devil, we must have the power of the Holy Ghost. Jesus told His disciples in Acts chapter 1 not to leave Jerusalem, but to wait for the Promise of the Father. He told them in chapter 1 verse 8, KJV "But you shall receive power when the Holy Spirit has come upon you; and you shall be witnesses to Me in Jerusalem, and in all Judea and Samaria, and to the end of the earth." Jesus told them to wait for the Holy Ghost because He knew the obstacles they were going to face. He knew the devil was out to get them, He knew that they were going to be lied on, talked about, be whipped, thrown in jail, left for dead, among other things and in order to keep on going in the faith, they were going to need the power of the Holy Ghost. Saints in these times today we need this same power, the power of the Holy Ghost. For we're living in times of a pandemic, we're living in times of recession, we're living in times of where people are shooting up churches, schools, grocery stores, and parades. We're living in a time where there's a war going on and in order for us to make it, in order for us not to throw in the towel then we must have the Holy Ghost.

Saints, we must realize that in order for us to make it, we must know the Word of God and we must have God living on the inside of us. We must have the Holy Ghost because it is absolutely essential for personal salvation. We need the Holy Ghost because we cannot do this on our own. Without God we are no match for the devil; with God we will throw in the towel when things get the worst, but with God we know that we can do all things through Christ who strengthens me.

So, I ask the question one more time: have you received the Holy Ghost since you believed? If the answer is no, I would lift up my hands and ask the Lord to fill me with the Holy Ghost. Why? Because you're going to need power to cast out the devil, power to speak those things that be not as though they are, power to lay hands on the sick, power to love your enemies, power to pray for those who despitefully use you, power to preach the gospel in session and out of season, power to run on and see what the end is going to be, power to walk right, power to talk right, power to do right, power to live holy. Lord fill us with Your power!

PRAYING IN THE HOLY GHOST

Saints must defend and promote the faith and resist false teachings. The way to do that is by building up ourselves in the most holy faith. Jude 1:20 (KJV), "But ye, building up yourselves on your most holy faith, praying in the Holy Ghost." The holy faith is the New Testament revelation handed down by Christ and the apostles. Those who are faithful to Christ Jesus are placed under the solemn obligation to "contend for the faith" that God delivered to the saints. Contending for the faith means taking a direct stand against those within the visible church who deny authority of the Bible. This requires study of God's word and a determined effort to know the truth and teaching of Scriptures. By praying in the Spirit, we must pray by the enabling power of the Holy Ghost, that is, by looking to the Holy Ghost to inspire, guide, energize, sustain, and help us to do battle in our praying.

The believer is powerless without the power of the Holy Ghost in his or her life. The Word tells us that he doesn't know how to pray as he ought to without the Holy Ghost. In order to have a power packed prayer life, we need and must have the indwelling of the Holy Ghost. The more time that Saints spend with God and His Spirit, the more he has of God's presence and His Power. The word tells the believer that once they receive the baptism of the Holy Ghost, they will receive power. That power will give them access to pray in the Holy Ghost. We cannot pray in the Holy Ghost if the Holy Ghost is not present with them. The release of the power of the Holy Ghost into the lives of the believers will cause them to pray in the Spirit with great boldness. Knowing that whatsoever they asked, God in faith, that it will come to pass.

Don't leave home without power! I believe that God wants the believer to have the same power the early church had. When James was killed and Peter was placed in jail, the church prayed in the Holy Ghost. Peter found himself in an impossible situation, for he was in jail, his hands and feet bound with 16 quaternions of soldiers all around him. Locked behind several doors, no way out, but God heard the prayers of the righteous that was going on all day and night. The prayers were so powerful that God sent an angel, who woke Peter up. Acts 12:7 (KJV), "And, behold, the angel of the Lord came upon him, and a light shined in the prison and he smote Peter on the side, and raised him up, saying, Arise up quickly. And his chains fell off from his hands. Praying in the Holy Ghost will give you victory in the face of defeat. Don't stop praying your situation is not over until God says that it's over.

THE SPIRIT OF GOD DWELLS IN YOU

Romans 8:8-9 (KJV), "So then they that are in the flesh cannot please God. But ye are not in the flesh, but in the Spirit, if so be that the Spirit dwells in you. Now if any man have not the Spirit of Christ, he is none of his."

If the Spirit of God dwells in you, all believers from the moment of their being saved or spiritual birth and faith in Jesus Christ have the Holy Ghost living in them. The indwelling presence of the Spirit is related to new birth; this baptism in the Spirit is an empowering experience and related to initiation into the inspiring or inspires devotion in others. Some of the things that the Spirit does as He lives in us–he sanctifies us, that is, cleanses, leads and motivate us into holy lives; delivering us from the bondage of sin; he tells us that we are the children of God and helps us that glorifies Christ; he guides us into oneness and close fellowship with our savior Jesus Christ. We need the power of the Holy Ghost in us to do the work of God.

POWER AGAINST UNCLEAN SPIRITS

Jesus wants His followers to wage war against the forces of evil by driving out evil spirits and healing the sick. " ...he gave them power against unclean spirits, to cast them out, and to heal all manner of sickness and all manner of disease," Matthew 10:1 (KJV). This demonstration of authority in spiritual confrontation is considered a continuing manifestation of the kingdom of God on earth. The kingdom is an assertion of God's power in action. The kingdom of God carries the idea of God coming into the world to assert His power, glory, and rights against Satan's dominion and the present systems of the world. "And as ye go, preach, saying, The kingdom of heaven is at hand," Matthew 10:7 (KJV).

An essential evidence that one is experiencing God's kingdom is a life of righteousness and peace, and joy in the Holy Ghost. The believer's responsibility is to persevere in diligently seeking God's kingdom in all its manifestations, hungering, and thirsting for God's presence and power both in their own lives and within the believer's community. It is Christ's purpose that the kingdom of heaven and its power be "at hand" to bring salvation, grace, and healing to God's people. When the kingdom of heaven is not being manifested among God's people, they should turn from the spirit of the world and all that is pleasing to God, "seek ... first the kingdom of God, and his righteousness," Matthew 6:33 (KJV) and pray "Thy kingdom come. Thy will be done," Matthew 6:10; Mark 9:29 (KJV).

PASTORS MUST LEAD
BY THE HOLY GHOST

Pastors are appointed by the Holy Ghost. Acts 20:28 (KJV), "Take heed therefore unto yourselves, and to all the flock, over the which the Holy Ghost hath made you overseers, to feed the Church of God, which he hath purchased with his own blood."

No church can function without a Pastor. In Acts 14:23, the book describes that certain individuals were appointed to the office of Pastor or overseer by Paul and Barnabas. They were spirit-filled missionaries who sought God's will through prayer and fasting in accordance with the spiritual qualifications, which were later established by the Holy Ghost in 1 Timothy 3:1-13 and Titus 1:5-9. Therefore, it is the Spirit who makes someone a Pastor or overseer in the church.

One of the major duties of overseers is to feed the sheet by teaching God's Word. They must always keep in mind that the flock given to them is no other than the people that God has purchased for Himself with His Son Jesus Christ precious blood. Likewise, overseers today must declare to their churches God's whole will. They must "preach the word in and out of season; reprove, rebuke, exhort with all long-suffering and doctrine (2 Tim 4:2) KJV; refuse to be preachers who seek to please people and say only what they want to hear (2 Tim 4:3). Pastors must protect the sheep from the enemies.

"For I know this, that after my departing all grievous wolves enter in among you, not sparing the flock," Acts 20:29 (KJV). Wolves influenced by ambition to build their own kingdoms or by the love of money, power, or popularity, imposters in the church will distort the original gospel as found in the New Testament. The true church consists of only those who by the grace of Jesus Christ and the word of God. Therefore, literally "keep awake" means "be on your guard." Overseers of God's people must always be sensitive to and watch out for those within their congregations who are not earnestly committed to the original message of Christ and the apostles. They must be so united with the Holy Ghost that they are carefully and tearfully concerned for their people, never stopping night and day to warn the flock about the danger facing them and ever pointing them to the only sure foundation, Jesus Christ and His word. The church that fails to share the Holy Ghost burning concern for church purity (Acts 20:18-35), refuses to maintain a firm stand for the truth, and refrains from disciplining those who undermine the authority of God's word, will soon cease to exist as a church. Paul sets an example for all of God's ministers–he never desires wealth or seeks to get rich from his work in the gospel. Paul had a great opportunity to get wealth. He had great influence among the people. He didn't do it because of the leading of the Holy Ghost, but because of the love for the gospel. Paul describes how he served as a shepherd of the church in Ephesus; he has declared the whole will of God by faithfully warning and teaching the Ephesian Christians (Acts 20:27). He says in Acts 20:26 (KJV), "Wherefore I take you to record this day, that I am pure from the blood of all men." What he was saying is that he exemplified a life before them; so, if they should die spiritually and be lost forever, Paul states that he would not be blamed because he was faithful in testifying about Christ. If the overseers do not want to be responsible for the perishing of those under their ministry, they must declare to them the whole will of God.

I Timothy 4:16 (KJV), "Take heed unto thyself, and unto the doctrine; continue in them: for in doing this thou shalt both save thyself, and them that hear thee." Living a holy life, remaining sensitive to the Spirit's operation and gifts, teaching sound doctrine, guarding the faith, and watching over one's spiritual life are more than a ministerial obligation for Timothy in this verse. These things are essential for his own salvation, future, and those whom he will minister to.

THE PRESENCE
OF GOD IN GREAT
DISTRESS

God understands our fears. We may feel afraid in our storms, but if we look to God, He will strengthen and encourage us. His Word is food for our souls in times of fear and darkness, and He offers His Holy Spirit to guide us through life's storms. Although we all experience spiritual barrenness at times, this is not the norm, for God desires to be near His people with help and comfort. Psalm 46:1 (KJV), "God is our refuge and strength, a very present help in trouble." This psalm expresses trust and confidence in God during a time of instability and insecurity. The power and ability to face the uncertainties and adversities of life are found in God. In Acts chapter 27, Paul walked in obedience and in the presence of the Lord, seeking to take his case to Rome and warning them of the danger ahead. They believed the owner of the ship rather than Paul. Sometimes we go through life storms for God to get the glory out of our lives. In verse 20, when hope was gone, they would be saved. The spirit spoke through Paul words of encouragement to them. God sent an angel to Paul in the night and reassured him that he would arrive at Rome to stand trial. This gave Paul great confidence in the midst of great danger at sea.

Every child of God must pray, "O Lord, I am thine, I serve thee; be my protector," Psalm 16:1-2 (KJV). Don't leave without power; this power of the Holy Ghost helped Paul navigate through this time of his life. Paul is a prisoner in the ship; nevertheless, he is a free man in Christ Jesus, living free from fear in God's presence while those who sail with are terrified because of the danger at sea. In this life, only the sincere and faithful believe and can experience the nearness of God's presence in the midst of life's dangers with courage and the blessed assurance in Christ.

THE WORK OF THE HOLY GHOST!

The Holy Ghost is the agency of sanctification that means being set apart for the Lord's use. At conversion, believers are indwelt by the Holy Ghost and come under His sanctifying influence. Some of the things that the Holy Ghost does He lives in us. He sanctifies, that is, cleanses, leads, and motivates us into holy lives, delivering us from the bondage of sin. He helps us in our worship of God. He produces Christlike graces of character that glorify Christ. Don't leave home without Him for He is our divine teacher, guiding us into all truth. He continually imparts God's love to us and gives us joy, comfort, and help. He leads us into oneness with Jesus Christ.

The Holy Ghost is the agent of service, empowering believers for service and witness. When we are baptized in the Spirit, we receive power to witness for Christ and work within the church and before the world (Acts 1:8). Throughout this church age, it is God's intended purpose that all believers experience baptism in the Holy Ghost. In the area of service, the Holy Ghost gives spiritual gifts to individual members of the church to edify, or strengthen the church. The Holy Ghost is the agent that God uses to incorporate believers into one body of Christ. To build the church, inspire church worship, to direct mission, appoint leaders and workers, give gifts to church, anointed preachers, protect the gospel and promote righteousness.

John 3:16 (KJV) states, "Howbeit when he, the Spirit of truth, is come, he will guide you into all truth: for he shall not speak of himself: but whatsoever he shall hear, that shall he speak: and he will shew you things to come." The convicting work of the Holy Ghost is not only directed towards the unsaved, but also the believers and the church in order to teach, correct, and guide them into all truth. The Holy Ghost will speak to believers concerning sin, the righteousness of Christ Jesus and the judgment of this evil world to conform them to Christ and His holy standard of righteousness. He will guide them into all truth, and glorify Christ. The Holy Ghost works within believers to reproduce Christ's holy life in their lives. If the Spirit filled believers reject the guidance of the Holy Ghost and are not convicted, they will be in condemnation. "We ought to obey God rather than man," Acts 5:29b (KJV). Further in Acts 5:32 (KJV) provides deeper understanding, "And we are his witness of these things; and so is also the Holy Ghost, whom God hath given to them that obey him." If there is no real obedience to Christ or a sincere seeking the righteousness of His kingdom, then any claim to possess the fullness of the Holy Ghost is not valid.

Pentecost without the lordship of Christ is impossible, for the Spirit in all His power is giving only to those living in obedience of God's word. One cannot be a real minister of the gospel without the work of the Holy Ghost in his or her lives. The spirit's work of convicting people of sin, righteousness, and judgment will be made known in all who are baptized in the Holy Ghost and are truly Spirit-filled believers. Any preacher or church that does not publicly expose sin and call for repentance and Biblical righteousness is not directed by the Holy Ghost. God's presence in the congregation is recognized by the exposure of the sin of unbelievers, that is, secret things of the heart, and their consequent convection and salvation.

The Holy Ghost does not speak of His own self or His own initiative. The Holy Ghost receives His message and instructions from Christ. John 16:14 (KJV), "He shall glorify me: for he shall receive of mine, and shall shew it unto you." The Holy Ghost takes that which is Christ's and reveals it to the believer. The Holy Ghost works within us to do what is necessary to awaken and deepen our awareness of Jesus' presence in our lives, drawing our hearts toward Him in faith, love, obedience, communion, worship, and praise. Don't leave home without power for you are going to need Him on your journey.

A PRAYER LIFE

The early church leader didn't move without the guidance of the Holy Ghost. The leaders knew they had power because the church had a prayer life. In the Book of Acts, throughout they were challenged in many areas, but they didn't have to be fearful because of the prayers. They had the threats against them, but they continued praying daily. They kept worshiping God in the Temple; they knew that the devil's plans would be defeated, so when they had prayed, the very place was shaken by the power of the Holy Ghost. They were empowered even more because they were all filled with the power of the Holy Ghost and began to speak with boldness and God used them in a mighty way.

The inner power of the spirit and the reality of God's presence brought about the filling of the Spirit, which frees the believers from fear of others and greatly increases the courage to speak out for God. The one essential cure to worry is prayer. Through prayer, we renew our trust in the Lord's faithfulness by casting all our problems and worries on Him who cares for us. Having a prayer life gives us the peace of God that will guard our hearts and minds as a result of communion with God. We must pray in the Spirit to combat the force of the devil. Prayer is not to be seen just as another weapon, but as part of the conflict itself– this is how the victory is for ourselves and others by working together with God, Himself. To fail to pray diligently, with all kinds of prayers in all situations, is to surrender to the enemy.

GREATER RURAL REACH: THE BACK STORY

In the year of two thousand and in the month of October, the Greater Hope Church of God in Christ was established. Earlier in March, the Lord laid on my heart to start a church in a rural East Texas town called Mount Pleasant. He gave me the scriptures from the King James version derived from Joshua 1:7-9, "Only be thou strong and very courageous. Be strong and of good courage; be not afraid neither be thou dismayed: for the Lord God is with thee whithersoever thou goest."

At a jail service that same month, God spoke once again through the scripture, James 4:10 (KJV), "Humble yourself in the sight of the Lord and He shall lift you up." Following the lead of the Holy Spirit, I approached our Jurisdictional Bishop, the Presiding Prelate, Bishop Frank W. Smith Jr., for his permission and his blessings. In July 2000, at the Holy Convocation of the Texas Northeast Third Ecclesiastical Jurisdiction, Bishop Smith granted it with great joy and with excitement. The vision was that Mount Pleasant was too large for only one Church of God in Christ.

After receiving the bishop's blessings, time, and great efforts for a place to worship began. I walked the neighborhoods evangelizing, praying, witnessing and passing out flyers of our soon to come opening of the Greater Hope Church of God in Christ. Souls were saved, healed and delivered. There was still no place of worship yet I was trusting and believing in the Lord Jesus that He would make a way. Months of searching, the Lord assured me again through the Holy Scripture, Joshua 1:9 (KJV), "Have I not commanded you? Be strong and courageous." Every step of the way, the Lord reassured me that He was with me. Sister Alma Tumey then offered us a building that she owned, which was the former Tumey Funeral Home. The building had been dormant for over 5 years and it was in need of a lot of work, but God worked it out. We found someone to renovate the building for $1,000 plus dollars and a local lumber company donated the carpet for free. With the building now presentable and still no pews, we set up folding chairs and got ready for church. On the fifth Sunday of October 2000, Dr. Francis Rundles, the founding pastor, along with his wife and three children opened up Greater Hope Church of God in Christ in Mount Pleasant, Texas. We started with 12 members and God blessed us. Later that year, a local church was remodeling their sanctuary and told us that we could have the choir seats, tables, and a lectern because the pews were promised out to someone else. But the minister who was to receive the pews, called and said that he did not want them and that we could have them for free. A donated pulpit lectern and communion cloth for the lectern and table and other wall decorations for the church were the finishing touches needed for the new church. On August 1, 2006, God blessed the church to purchase a portion of property and again on October 10, 2006, we were able to purchase additional lots adjacent to the first portion of property on Hayes Street in Mount Pleasant, Texas. God continued to bless Greater Hope Church of God in Christ to purchase property on West 10th and Elyse Street on November 14, 2008, which is now our present location.

In the year of 2010, God blessed us to make great strides and steps in the first stages of our new building. May 2012, God blessed us to get our new church and the building process began. On the first Sunday in December 2012, Greater Hope Church of God in Christ had their first service in the new building. Since we have been in this building, we have been blessed to start new ministries such as the Couples Ministry, the local Evangelist team, the Brotherhood, the Real Talk with Dr. Rundles where teenagers are given a platform to deal with their problems and issues, to name a few. God has blessed us with many new members and has added several ministers and a church mother. Out of this ministry, one received his minister's license. At the July 2014 Texas Northeast Third

Convocation, I, Dr. Francis Rundles, was promoted under the leadership of the late Bishop T.W. Johnson to the office of Superintendent of the Faith Temple District, which is now the Greater Hope Outreach District. In May 2015, we were blessed again to do an extension to our fellowship area and add a concrete driveway and additional parking. During the summer of 2016, Greater Hope added covers over our south and east doors. This is our 23rd year and we're continuing on in God's grace.

GROWING CHURCHES
IN THE RURAL OR
RURAL REACH

In regards to church size, the definition of 'small' means a church with less than 200 members, and the term 'rural' means a town of less than 10,000 people. You probably hear about the larger churches adding thousands of members every year, but where does this leave the Pastor of a church of forty in a community of 500 people? When God sends a shepherd, He always has a flock to be shepherd.

What does church growth mean in such a congregation?

Experience has convinced me that there are principles that will help the small, rural churches grow and have a vital ministry.

1. Principles= Understanding Hindrances to Growth
    You must understand some of the dynamics of the rural church.
    Consider some of the things most important in these churches.

    A. Traditions: Some are beneficial and others severely hinder the church's ministry, but in a rural church almost all are considered sacred.
    B. History: Many of these rural churches are afraid to look to the future, but they recall a glorious past.

2. Rural Reach= Growth Occurs When Vision and Values Match

    A. Their vision and values match.
    B. Their lifestyle and lip service match.
    C. Their conduct and character match.
    D. Their image and integrity match.
    E. Their promise and production match.
    F. Their strategy and support match.

3. Reaching the masses by any means necessary (Matthew 9:35-38) and willing to do whatsoever it takes means having a heart of compassion— loving the people.

HOW TO GROW A CHURCH IN THE RURAL!

Questions to consider when reaching out into the community and compelling them to come. (Luke 14:23)

1. What kind of impact are we having on this godless city?
2. Do we have an outreach program in our local church?
3. It appears that we are weak in outreach to our own Jerusalem. We are so busy with the work of the church that we've lost contact with lost people.

Matthew 9:36 (KJV), "Lord give us the heart of compassion." We need to see as Jesus saw and feel as Jesus felt so that we will do as Jesus did. A great need for lost people. Jesus saw lost people as distressed. The word means "troubled or irritated." It points to the load of problems that people apart from Christ bear. Jesus saw lost people as dispirited. The word means, "downcast or thrown down." It points to the utterly helpless and forsaken condition of people who are lost in sin without the Savior. Jesus saw lost people as a sheep without a shepherd. Jesus saw the great harvest of souls. In Matthew 9:37 (KJV), it referenced that the harvest is plentiful and this was an important concept that Jesus wanted his disciples to grasp. Jesus saw the great need for workers: God uses saved people to save others.

And if you are thinking, but I am not a minister, you don't understand. The workers in the Lord's harvest are not just those in position of ministry; rather, they are those who have tasted of God's salvation telling others of what He has done in your life. Or, as a beggar telling another beggar where we can get bread. "The harvest is truly plenteous ..." Matthew 9:37 (KJV). Pray for us; pray for labour's; "Finally, brethren pray for us, that the word of the Lord may have free course, and be glorified even as it is with you:" 2 Thessalonians 3:1 (KJV).

In Acts 1, we are reminded of what is to come when you receive the power from the Holy Ghost. In vs. 8 (KJV) "But ye shall receive power, after that the Holy Ghost is come upon you:" Power means more than strength or ability; it designates especially power in operation, in action. The release of the power of the Holy Ghost in Acts, in and through the believers' lives, caused them to witness with all boldness, with great power, with many signs, wonders, and miracles.